How to Sell on Etsy With Facebook

Selling on Etsy Made Ridiculously Easy Vol.1

by Charles Huff
Founder, Craft Biz Insider

Published in USA by: Craft Biz Insider

Charles Huff

© Copyright 2018

ISBN-13: 978-1-970119-19-0
ISBN-10: 1-970119-19-5

Table of Contents

About the Author

Charles Huff is a former cubicle drone turned full-time Etsy seller.

He is also the owner of the world's most neurotic Jack Russell Terrier.

A Special FREE Gift for You!

If you'd like FREE instant access to my special report "Top 10 Marketing Tools Every Etsy Seller Should Use" then head over to **CraftBizInsider.com/Free.**

(What else you gonna do? Watch another "Twilight" movie?!)

Prologue: How Etsy Sellers Can Actually Make Money With Facebook

"In order to be irreplaceable, one must always be different."

-Coco Chanel

Facebook saved my life.

Well, not literally.

It's not like Mark Zuckerberg came flying through the window, dressed in tights, to rescue me from a burning building.

But close...

Because until I found Facebook, the Etsy store my mom and I ran was floundering. Hemorrhaging.

Losing money by the decorative truckload.

In the early days all you had to do was set up Etsy shop, post pretty pictures, and wait for the flood of hungry customers to burst through your virtual doors. (Ah, how I miss you, 2010.)

Soon, things got a lot more crowded on the Etsy street corner, once everybody with a craft room set up their store…

Suddenly just to stay afloat you had to pay the Google pay-per-click (PPC) mafia to get traffic to your Etsy store, plus you had to rent banner space on every weird niche blog you could find.

Our handcraft business, started in my mom's garage back in 1982, was my mom's only source of income, and it would have disappeared like so many other small-business ventures.

But then we found Facebook, and everything changed.

Not at first, mind you. I made EVERY

Facebook marketing mistake you can make. I either posted too much, or not enough.

My pictures were vague and oddly sized, my call-to-actions unclear, my fan count hovering at a miserable 154.

And then I turned to one of the foremost Facebook marketing experts in the country: my 22-year-old cousin.

Forget all those social media "experts." I needed somebody who lived, breathed, liked, swallowed and dreamed of Facebook.

Because I knew Facebook is where my buyers LIVED.

Everything my cousin taught me — such as how to get comments & likes and turn a fan page into a 24-hour cash machine — I will teach you.

You don't even have to buy my cousin a Carna Asada burrito, like I had to.

However, before we get into the nitty-gritty of Facebook marketing (and there's a lot of nitty and gritty) I want to make sure you get a good, big-picture look at Facebook marketing…and what it can ACTUALLY do for us as Etsy sellers.

And why it's too easy to fail at Facebook marketing.

The Trouble With Facebook

Most marketers have a difficult time making money with Facebook. This is because:

- Facebook users hate to LEAVE the Facebook universe.
- Facebook users like nothing that "smells" like marketing.
- Facebook users are getting harder and harder to reach with Facebook's constant algorithm. (Algorithm is just a fancy way of saying "Facebook wants you to pay to get noticed.")

But here's a few awesome and cool things as an Etsy seller:

- We DON'T have to force users to leave

Facebook to buy our stuff

- Etsy stores don't feel like hard-sell sales-y crap. (It feels like art, which it is.)
- Pictures of our beautiful creations get shared…a lot. This makes it much, much easier to crack the Facebook news feed

So, if you've tried Facebook in the past and had limited results, or you're just plain skeptical about Facebook being of any benefit to you, just realize for EVERYBODY ELSE Facebook is a royal pain in the butt to make any money with.

But for us Etsy sellers, Facebook can become a steady and lucrative source of traffic and leads. (And if done well, it can save an Etsy business that's on the edge of oblivion.)

Yeah, But How Do You Make Money With Facebook?

There are four different ways to monetize your Facebook page as Etsy sellers:

1. Have visitors claim Facebook offers straight from your Page.

2. Send people from your Fan Page to your Etsy store.
3. Send people from your Fan Page to your website.
4. Turn "fans" into email subscribers (who you can market to repeatedly).

And here's the cool part: you can do these all at once.

You can — and should — have an app that lets people buy your wares right there on your website. You should also post interesting content, in the form of photos, videos and other good stuff that will point people back to your Etsy storefront.

You should also have some way to capture those eyeballs in a way that lets you market to them repeatedly.

And email still beats all those hip social media platforms for continual marketing opportunities.

The Secret to Marketing Your Etsy Store on Facebook

The absolute number one secret to real success

on Facebook isn't in the size of your ad budget, it isn't in the quality of your product photos, it isn't in the level of deep discounts you offer, and it isn't in the number of likes and fans you have.

The secret is about making the "experience" of buying your stuff fun. People don't just buy for the product, they buy for the story they can tell their friends about that cool, new Etsy handcraft they found.

And their newfound status as a hip purveyor of DIY artistic culture.

And nothing tells a story — your story as a creative artist — than Facebook.

So don't worry too much about the technical details. There are quite a few of them; that's just how social platforms work.

Just remember to:

- Tell your story
- Make it fun
- Make it easy

Do those three things and you'll have so much

success you might just end up writing your own book on Facebook marketing for Etsy sellers. (I can't wait to read it!)

Chapter 1:
4 Keys to Creating a Killer Facebook Presence

"Do the thing and you will have the power"

-Ralph Waldo Emerson

Notice I didn't say "Creating a Killer Facebook Page."

As I will try to make clear throughout this book, the idea of your Facebook Page being the ultimate destination -- where you do much of your Etsy wheeling-and-dealing is pretty much gone.

Unless things change by the time I type this sentence.

These days a Facebook page is more a branding piece. Something that gives would-be customers a quick snapshot of the personality of a company.

Look at the Facebook page for Coca-Cola - Facebook.com/CocaColaUnitedStates

Aside from pictures of ridiculously thin models consuming carbonated beverages there's little HERE that gives you the opportunity to buy Coke.

And that's okay.

The modern Facebook Page is the road sign telling people WHERE you'd like them to go. It isn't the destination where you want people to end up.

This is a shift from how things used to be before 2016.

But if you can take that to heart, and work within those parameters, you'll find quicker (and more affordable) results with your Facebook marketing.

So, here are 4 Keys to Creating a Killer Facebook Presence for your Etsy brand:

Key #1: Create Your Page (and Claim Your Name)

I know this is gonna come as a shock. But you have to create a Facebook page to use a Facebook page.

Shocking, I know.

And yet I still know Etsians who continue to do most of their Facebook activities through their personal Facebook profile.

Which is fine...I guess...

But you miss out on a lot of promotional opportunities available to you when you don't have your own Facebook page.

The process is sim-ple:

- Head over to: https://www.facebook.com/pages/create/.
- Choose "Business or Brand" or "Community or Public Figure." (Take a wild stab which one you should choose.)
- Choose a category. Don't stress too much

about these. I think "Arts and Crafts Store" is probably a good choice for any Etsian. But you want to pick one that most defines your shop.

- Come up with a page name

- Come up with a username

Hold on! Page Name? Username?

What in tarnation is going on here?

Don't worry.

WHAT'S IN A NAME

Here's what you gotta know:

- Username refers to the actual name in the URL. (Example: Facebook.com/DelightfulDesertDecorations)
- Page Name refers to the name people see below your profile photo

Couple things to keep in mind:

- You can change your Facebook Page Name as many times as you want. (But only once every seven days.)
- You can change your username ONCE after you get 25 likes. (It'll start off as something ugly like Facebook.com/DelightfulDecorations48399).
- You can "ask" to have your username changed, after the initial change. But it can be a pain to do.

And what names should you go with?

For Usernames try to stick with your shop name. If that's gone, and it might be, try adding "The" or "the Real" or "Inc."

Facebook is not great about protecting proprietary names. So, do your best.

For Page Names, I like to go with [SHOP NAME] + [KEYWORDS] - Something like [BOB'S HOUSE OF SOAP - Organic Gluten-Free Handmade Soap]

But wait! Keywords?

Nobody said anything about keywords?

THE STRANGE WORLD OF
Keywords

Here's what you need to know about keywords:

• **They are the semantic phrases people type in to look for stuff.** "Shabby chic"; "Victorian dolls"; "Craft room decorations."

• **Humans over robots.** Yes, you want to find the most popular keywords. But only if they would appeal to would-be human customers. Don't just do it because Google said you should.

• **Find 2-3 keywords.** Put the most accurate and popular one in your Page name. The rest you'll put elsewhere in your Facebook page profile. (More on that in a second.)

And where do you find these keywords?

By heading over to the Google Keyword planner. All you do is:

- Google the phrase "Google Keyword Planner"
- Put in a description of the type of craft you create
- Sort the results (by clicking the top) by # of searches per month
- Find the top 2-3 search phrases.

For example, let's say I run a shop that creates lamps out of antique pieces. And I might think that "vintage floor lamps" is absolutely the best description of my stuff.

But I might notice that "antique lamps" wasn't as popular as "vintage floor lamps." Hmmm….interesting. (Not something I would have expected.)

In that case, we might want to do a page name of "Al's Lamps - Vintage Floor Lamps for Every Occasion." And that's how I would do it: your "branded" store name followed by a description containing a keyword.

Unless you already have a keyword in your branded store name. You might just be that awesome.

Key #2: Fill Your Page With Keywords

You've already got the keywords. Now it's time to put them in important areas of your Facebook ecosystem.

That includes:

- About section
- Short Description
- Long Description (sometimes called the "impressum")
- Company overview
- Mission
- Products
    - But don't stop there. Other good places for your 2-3 keywords include:
    - Pinterest profile
    - Twitter bio
    - Instagram bio
    - YouTube channel descriptions
    - Website

Anywhere else you can think of

The goal is to tell the Google bots that your

Facebook Page, and the rest of your connected marketing platform, is ABOUT these 2-3 keyword phrases.

Do that and Google might just reward you with some serious (and free) promotion.

Key #3: Add Some Compelling Profile Photos

There are two key profile photos that can make the difference between your page looking sad and lonely or vibrant and awesome.

The first is the Facebook timeline cover photo -- the BIG header photo at the top of your page.

Though it's a HUGE part of your Facebook real estate, many Etsians don't use this space to full advantage.

The Timeline Cover Photo

Here are a few key points to keep your cover photo looking sharp and awesome:

- **Your cover photo needs to apply to your Etsy business.** For Etsians this means showcasing a product, a design or a theme that coincides with what you're trying to sell. Replicate the "vibe" of your Etsy business on your Facebook page.
- **Get super creative!** Your cover photo needs to dazzle your visitors. Hire a freelance graphic designer (check out Upwork.com) or use your own creative skill to come up with something. (The FREE tool PicMonkey is a great addition to your graphic arsenal.) Just remember the Timeline Cover Photo needs to be 851 x 315 pixels.
- **Choose warm colors that contrast Facebook's scheme.** This means avoid the BLUES that seem to pervade everything Facebook does. (You know, because Mark Zuckerberg is color blind.) Contrast will make your cover photo stick out and catch the eye. (Go with oranges and reds.)
- **One of the best ways to catch the eye is to include pictures of people.** For instance, say you make jewelry or clothing for your Etsy shop, display a

timeline cover photo that shows people wearing your products. Closeups are great if relevant.

- **Place a "tag-line" or a testimonial on the cover photo.** If someone gives you a fantastic testimonial about how they love what you're doing, slap it on there. It not only adds to your credibility, but another factor that may keep the visitor on your page.
- **Events or something special going on?** Got a special sale or a live event going on? (Or maybe you sold your 100th item?) Tailor a special cover photo just for that.

Your Facebook cover photo is your store's billboard. (Without having to pay thousands of dollars for that ad real estate over the freeway.) So, use it wisely.

Facebook Profile Photo

Your profile photo, or thumbnail photo, will show up on more than just your page. This photo will make its way into the Facebook News Feed and internal graph search.

Think of your Timeline cover photo as your hook and your profile photo as your bait.

Making an irresistible profile photo is an important part of this equation. (And one that many Etsians mess up.)

Perhaps the most basic aspect about your profile photo is that it needs to look professional! But not staged and fake, like a stock photo. Geez, sounds pretty hard. What are we supposed to do?

To get a fantastic looking profile photo, here are a few tips:

- Remember how photos of people attract people? The same goes for your profile photo. A shot of a person is almost always better than a shot of anything else.
- Needs to be visible at a small size. Try not to get your entire craft room or every product you sell in your thumbnail.
- Make it about one clear THING…and let the viewer's imagination take over.
- Pictures over text. Put your text-heavy

logo somewhere else. Find a photo and stick with it.

Key #4: Fill Your Facebook Timeline With Juicy Awesomeness

If your profile photo was the bait, and your cover photo was the hook…then your initial Timeline posts should be the tug that brings them into the boat.

Okay, enough of the shoddy fishing analogy. Let's get down to business.

What should be in your Timeline?

Well…this is where many businesses, not just Etsy stores, fall short. They try to wrench every ounce of promotional potential out of their Facebook timeline. Not realizing that most would-be customers don't want to be sold to…

…they want to be invited to a party.

Is there a way you could transform your Facebook timeline — the content that fills your Facebook page — from boring marketing to a party atmosphere?

I don't mean "Doing keg stands in Mexico" type of party.

But somewhere that looks fun and that people want to be a part of. Could you create content in your Facebook timeline around the following questions:

- What made you start your Etsy business?
- What influences your designs?
- Who are you?
- What are your current successes in the business?
- Introduce any other craftsmen, designers or artists on your team.
- Announce any new projects you may work on.
- Share the struggles you may face...use this one in moderation...don't break into a sob story. Be sure to always come up with awesome solutions that fill people with hope. Humans are suckers for happy endings.

Notice how none of these FEEL like overt

selling. And yet…

…each of them lay the groundwork for some nice, future sales. And moving all this Facebook activity into futures sales is what we'll tackle in the next chapter.

Chapter 1 Action Steps:

- **Create your page and claim your name.** Try to get your store name in your username. And for your page name, use a combination of your store name and popular keywords people use to find your type of crafts.

- **Fill your page with keywords.** Not just in the page name, but also look at the about section, short description, company overview, mission and products.

- **Add compelling profile photos.** For your Timeline cover photo make sure it has warm colors that contrast with the Facebook color scheme. And include people, if you can. For the profile photo avoid text-heavy logos and go with headshots.

- **Fill your Facebook Timeline with awesomeness.** Things like influences, new projects, stories about your process...even struggles you've had. All

of this can make you much more
relatable.

Chapter 2:
How to Take Your Facebook Marketing to 11!

"Though we travel the world over to find the beautiful, we must carry it with us or we find it not."

-Ralph Waldo Emerson

Man, it used to be so easy.

If you were reading an earlier version of this book – way back in the Mesozoic era – this is the part of the book where I would tell you how to outfit your Facebook page with some apps and let the Etsy sales roll in.

Boy, that didn't last long.

Couple things happened:

- Facebook changed the entire look and feel of their Facebook pages
- Facebook de-emphasized the "Fan Page" as a destination and made the "News Feed" the place to be
- Facebook became a "pay-to-play" marketing platform

And by "pay-to-play," I mean unless you "pay" your posts don't have a prayer of getting any "play."

What does this mean for us Etsians?

It means focusing our energy on making the prettiest, whiz-bang Fan Page in the entire world is not the end-all, be-all goal it used to be.

Though that is a nice side benefit.

Instead, the NEW goal is to create bite-sized nuggets of consumable Facebook content that not only show up in a potential customer's newsfeed – and get them to stop playing Kandy Krush for 12 seconds – but eventually get them to head over to online locations that can actually make us money, like our Etsy store or our website.

This doesn't mean you can't have instant success selling your crafts right there on Facebook. I have and continue to do. In a later chapter I'll show you how to do this with Facebook offers.

It just means that in order to make sure the time, energy and money you spend on Facebook bears fruit it REALLY helps to have some important foundational pieces set up in your marketing funnel.

It isn't EASY, and it won't happen overnight, but if you take the time to set up the 6 Pillars I will recommend in this chapter, you will bring much-needed predictability to your Facebook marketing.

And with predictability — and the right systems in place — comes more sales.

Thoroughly discouraged, yet? Freaking out that things have changed?

Don't worry. It's not that bad.

It just requires a mindset shift. From seeing Facebook less as a clubhouse or party location – like it used to be – and more like a toll booth operator.

If you want to get access to their more than 2.3 Gazillion Facebook users you will have to figure out how to cajole, persuade and bribe Facebook to let you through.

And how to do that regularly is what we'll strive toward in this chapter.

With all that said -- "is he ever going to get to the point?" -- here are 6 Pillars of Facebook Awesomeness to get your Etsy marketing funnel set up the right (and profitable) way:

Pillar #1: A Facebook Business Manager Account

If the extent of your Facebook marketing, to this point, has been to publish a post and then hit "boost post," you are missing out on a HUGE part of the Facebook marketing possibilities out there for you.

But don't blame yourself. Facebook doesn't make it easy.

Their interface of Business Manager is just

slightly less daunting than a Tax Code manual. And they keep changing the name — and look — of their business page interface. ("Do I use the Power Editor or the Ads Manager or the Facebook Business Manager? Are they all the same thing?")

Here's what ya gotta do:

- Head over to business.facebook.com/create and select "Create Account"
- Confirm your identity and login
- Create your business account

Head over to CraftBizInsider.com/FBBiz101 to get a detailed walk-through of how to make this happen.

You might be saying…

Okay, Charles, but WHY do I have to create a Business Manager account?

I don't need to run multiple Facebook pages. I don't have a staff that will handle my Facebook marketing for me.

And, last time I checked, I didn't run a marketing

agency.

Good questions.

The BIG reasons you want to sign up for a Business Manager account are that:

- You'll be able to create far more sophisticated/awesome Facebook ads (more on that later) than you would otherwise
- You'll be able to generate a Facebook Retargeting Pixel

That last one is the important one. This will allow you to show pictures of your creations to people who have visited your website.

Even when they're NOT on your website.

This is HOW you can visit the Target website, looking for a set of bar stools, and suddenly everywhere you go you see ads for Target barstools.

Creepy? Yes.

Super-effective? You bet.

But we'll cover all of that in more detail LATER.

For now, just know creating a Facebook Business Manager account is like flossing. It may not seem important, now, but you'll regret it later if you don't do it.

Pillar #2: Website Goodies

I will assume you have a website. Please, oh please, tell me you have a website.

Whether it's one of those done-for-you kinds — such as Wix or SquareSpace — or a more custom-built site — such as using a WordPress theme — you want to have marketing real estate you OWN.

Real Estate that you're NOT renting from the Etsy landlords.

NOTE: I wrote an entire book about setting up your Etsy store website. You can check it out at: CraftBizInsider.com/Blogging

Okay, so what goodies do you need/want on your website?

There are FOUR important ones:

- **A Facebook retargeting pixel** - If what I said sounds like a foreign language, don't worry. There are plenty of people, for cheap, who can install this for you. All it is is a tiny piece of HTML code -- stay with me -- that you (or somebody more tech-y) places on the HEADER of your website. This is what will allow you to track how successful your Facebook ads are as well as serve ads to people EVEN when they aren't on your website. (Cool stuff!)

- **A Piece of Your Etsy Store on Your Website** - How complex or simple this is will depend on how your website is set up. I like to use the Etsy 360 app, which reproduces elements of my Etsy store on my website. Another tool I like is the Advanced Etsy Widget. But this only works if your website is running on WordPress. But you could also sell direct from your site, using a tool such as WooCommerce. Just know you must deal with some payment processing headaches. But it can be worth it financially.

- **A "Welcome Picture" On the Front Page -** This isn't mandatory, and I don't know how much it will boost your income, but I like websites that have a picture of the artist/owner on the home page. Personalizes it for me, and I think it personalizes it for other people too. (Too shy to show yourself on camera? Then just have a close-up picture of your hands working on your crafts.)

- **An Email Opt-In Landing Page -** Like it sounds this is a page where you do just one thing: ask people to opt-in to your email list. I use the tool LeadPages, a landing page template creator which produces beautiful pages. But you can use other tools such as Instapage. (Or even get a designer to make one for you cheap.) What you want is to create a page that has website navigation removed. Just a picture, an enticement to sign up (maybe a coupon) and a place for people to leave their email address. Simple, but powerful.

But how are you going to collect those email addresses? I'm so glad you asked...

Pillar #3: An Email Collector

The marketing types call these auto-responders. But I prefer email collectors. Sounds less like something you'd see under a car engine.

What this software does is allow you to collect email addresses in databases and then send those subscribers pre-written follow-up email messages and future one-off broadcast emails.

There are a LOT of companies that offer this service. The one I just shifted to last year — and love — is ConvertKit. But there are also companies like Aweber, MailChimp, and iContact. (Some FREE, some not.)

Most of them have a FREE trial. So, give each a try and see which one has the interface you like best, and go with that one.

And once you do that you want to create...

Pillar #4: Some Follow-Up Emails

Don't worry. These don't have to be long emails

the size of Moby Dick.

I would just start out with THREE follow-up emails. This is what I like to do:

Email 1 - The "Here's Your Free Thing-Y"

This is simple. this is an email where you give them the THING they get for signing up for your list. Maybe it's a coupon.

Or maybe it's a tutorial on how to make a craft. Whatever it is, in this email you give them the THING-y. And you send this email right after they sign up. No delays.

Email 2 - The "What Inspires Me" Email (2 Days Later)

This is an email where you talk about your creative inspiration. Maybe a little about your process; why you create what you create.

Don't need to hard-sell here. Just give them an insight into how your artistic creations come to life. And at the end of this email, ask them a question: "What inspires you? I'd love to know."

This is a great way to engage with your subscribers and ensure that your future emails get delivered to them.

Email 3 - The "Did You Check This Out?" Email (2 Days Later)

This is the email where you send them to your Etsy store. Tell them you're really excited about your latest offerings. And ask for their feedback.

People love to give feedback.

You're not overtly selling, but you will make a ton of sales. Especially after you give them a coupon code.

But more important, you're making them feel like a part of the process.

If they bought stuff, encourage them to share it on social media. (Maybe even mention there's a contest for everybody who buys something and shares a picture.)

Setting up your funnel this way will help ensure that all your Facebook Marketing has a real impact on your business. Not just a waste of time.

And making sure that people on Facebook see your funnel is what we'll discuss in the next chapter.

Chapter 2 Action Steps:

- **Sign up for Facebook Business Manager.** Offers you a lot more promotional flexibility than just running a Facebook page straight from your profile.

- **Get some goodies on your website.** Those goodies include a Facebook retargeting pixel (for future advertising), your Etsy store embedded on your site, a landing page to collect email addresses, and welcoming picture of you.

- **Sign up for an email collector.** You want to be able to collect email addresses and send out pre-written email messages.

- **Write three follow-up emails for new subscribers.** The first one will give them something, such as a coupon or discount. The second one will tell them what inspires you. The third will let them know what new creations you've got in your Store.

Chapter 3: How to Crack the Facebook News Feed

"By being yourself, you put something wonderful in the world that was not there before."

-Edwin Elliot

The title of this chapter is misleading.

That's because the only thing you need to CRACK the Facebook newsfeed is unlimited amounts of ad budget. Spend enough money and you'll crack even the most difficult of newsfeeds.

And if that describes you, then don't worry about it. You've got this covered.

But unless you have Kardashian in your last name -- or own a private island in the Tropics -- then chances are you must do things a little more bootstrapp-y.

You'll need to create content that has a HIGH LIKELIHOOD of cracking the Facebook newsfeed.

So when it is discovered by someone in your ideal customer demographic -- either through a paid ad or referred to them by one of their friends or simply because they were checking out your Facebook page -- then it has a GOOD CHANCE of making a serious connection.

And make enough of those connections, and build up brand equity, then you have a great chance of making not just a sale but acquiring a long-term customer.

The TRICK is to create content that doesn't feel like MARKETING. But actually is.

Impossible? Unrealistic? Beyond your capabilities?

Hardly.

Just requires you have a Facebook content plan that ensures you check all the important business boxes. (Luckily, I have just the plan for you.)

So, here's my 4-step process for creating compelling Facebook content that will crack the newsfeed:

Step #1: Commit to Doing Less Facebook Content Than You Think You Should

I know this will be tough for you to swallow -- even harder to implement -- but I will ask you to do LESS when it comes to Facebook.

That's right. I want you to do LESS than you think you have to do.

Content that is.

In the good, old days of Facebook Marketing -- you know, back in 2012 -- the rule of thumb was to update your Facebook page with new posts 1-2x a day.

This was good advice -- and the advice I used to give in this very book -- when you had a good chance of 60-70% of your fans seeing your content.

Them days are long gone.

These days, unless your fans are engaged with your page, less than 10% of your Fan base can reliably be counted on to see your stuff.

Maybe even less.

Which means: there is no upside to exhausting yourself by creating 5-7 piece of content, maybe more, for a platform that gives you no incentive to do so.

Instead, I recommend you focus your energy on two scheduled posts a week, one an actual piece of content on your website and the other a post trying to boost engagement. (You can post more if you've got a special offer going.)

My approach looks like:

- **One quality piece of content.** This could be a blog post, a video, a cool set of photos of your new creation. An inspirational quote next to a beautiful photo. Whatever. You will then super-charge that content's reach by buying a cheap $5 ad "boosting" it to your fan base and any other groups -- such as fans of other Etsy stores -- you think might be interested.

- **One "question" post.** The point of this content is to get people to respond. I like to do things like "What have you got planned this weekend?" "What inspires your creativity?" Stuff like that. But you could also put up a picture of two new products and ask: "How much do you think these should cost?" "Which do you like best?" "What would you call this creation?"

Step #2: Focus Your Energy at the End of the Week

Sounds good. Two posts of content. And the occasional promotional post. But WHEN is the best time to post this?

Generally, I've found, the end of the workweek, Thursday and Friday afternoons, are the best times to post.

So, my schedule looks something like this.

- Thursday 4pm - Piece of Content (Spend $5-$15 boosting my post)
- Friday 3pm - Question post (Anything you can think of to get people talking)
- Saturday 11am - Anything that links to my store

It's important that you do it in this order. The piece of content gets people EXPOSED to your brand. The question post gets people ENGAGED with your brand.

And when you are ready to sell something, you put out something that lets people JOIN the tribe of your brand.

I can't guarantee this will work for every Etsian. But it's worked for me and I think it will work for you.

Step #3: Create a Content Calendar

Worry not. I will not ask you to break any news scoops.

Unless you want to.

But to stay consistent with your content

production, and make sure you get the biggest bang for your content buck, it can be super-helpful to have a content calendar that lays out what you'll be creating and when.

Elsie and Emma over at A Beautiful Mess kindly shared a picture of their Blog Post Planning Marker Board. (To check it out, head over to CraftBizInsider.com/beautifulmessblog.)

And while you don't have to create as much content as they do -- they are machines -- I do think their process can give you some ideas about how to structure your own content.

For example, if you look at their board you'll see topics such as:

- Places We Love
- Halloween Milkshakes
- Fireplace Display
- Ghost Decor
- Scarf Styles x6
- Ghost Pinata Party
- 3 Bears Costume
- Food TBD
- Giveaway
- Modern Dress

It's a good mix of holiday-themed stuff -- this was obviously created in October -- but also interesting stuff they think their audience would like.

My calendar is far-less ambitious, I'm loath to admit, but it looks something like this:

- **Week 1:**
- Th/Inspirational quote
- F/Question: Weekend plans

- **Week 2:**
- Th/Behind the scenes video
- F/Question: Creative process
- Sa/Product promotion - Coupon, Special offer, or Contest

- **Week 3:**
- Th/Inspirational quote
- F/Question: This or That? (Milk chocolate or dark chocolate? Beatles or Stones? Thor or Iron Man?)

- **Week 4:**
- Th/Photos of new creations; "From the Lab"
- F/Question: What's your favorite? (Gangster movie? Cheesy book? Reality show?)

You'll notice I don't promote heavily. Not because I'm a nice person, but because it doesn't work.

Instead, I recommend you focus MOST of your energy on making feel connected to your brand. And then when you are ready to sell something, they are most assuredly ready to buy.

Step #4: Get Some Professional Help

No, not that kind of professional help. Not that there's anything wrong with that.

I mean the "Boy, it'd be nice if somebody could help me out with some of this content stuff."

We're going to go over tools and apps that can help this whole Facebook marketing thing in a later chapter.

But at some point, after you've been doing this for a while, you will start to hit a wall.

You're either going to run out of questions to ask or run out of quotes you want to share. And that's when it's good to get a Virtual Assistant to help you out for an hour a two or week.

What you have them will depend on what you need.

I've had my assistant:

- Scour other Facebook pages for good questions to ask
- Collect inspirational quotes in a Google spreadsheet
- Schedule and publish all my Facebook posts
- Reply to all people who answer a question
- Edit my photos in Canva or PicMonkey to make them look awesome
- Share that same content on all my other social channels (Pinterest, Twitter, Instagram)
- Publish a press release about my new

listings

And this doesn't have to be a HUGE expenditure. (I have an assistant, based in the Philippines, who helps for two hours @ $8/hr. Best $16 I spend all week.)

Part of you might resist this. And that's okay. I resisted it too.

But there's something powerful about getting a fresh eye on your marketing. If you find the right person -- Upwork is a good place to go -- then you'll have somebody who doesn't just DO the job you ask them to do. But offer ideas on HOW to reach even more people than you thought possible.

And reaching more people, and getting more Facebook fans and email subscribers, is what we'll discuss in the next chapter.

Chapter 3 Action Steps:

- **Commit to doing less.** The days of posting every day on Facebook are gone. Better to create 1-2 pieces of good content rather than 5-7 pieces of mediocre content.

- **Focus your energy at the end of the week.** Thursday - Saturday are the busiest days on Facebook. So, gear up for those days.

- **Create a content calendar.** Doesn't have to be elaborate. Just something that helps keep you on track.

- **Get professional help.** A virtual assistant can help gather quotes, edit photos, schedule posts...even respond to comments. (Saving you a lot of time.)

Chapter 4:
How to Get Thousands of
Fans in Just Minutes a Day

"There's not a word yet, for old friends who've just met."

-Jim Henson

"There's not a word yet,
for old friends who've just met."
-Jim Henson

Here's where all that hard work you did in the earlier chapters pays off…and that's by growing your Facebook fan base into a legion of die-hard enthusiasts and future customers.

But, hold on!

Didn't I earlier say Facebook wasn't the ultimate destination for your marketing?

That getting a bunch of "Facebook fans" for your page isn't worth it.

That spending oodles of money on your fans is wasted effort.

Yes and no.

The actual worth of a SINGLE Facebook fan is negligible. That person may or may not know who the heck your business is or ever buy a single thing from you. They may not even be the person.

But just as getting your book onto the New York Times Bestseller List can be a big boost in credibility when you're an author, so can having a decent number of fans - usually about 500-1000 fans at least -- for your Facebook Page go a long way toward establishing your brand as something people want to buy from.

So, here are my FOUR Tips for getting a ton of Facebook fans in just minutes a day:

Fan Booster Tip No.1: Ask/Beg Everybody You Know to Like Your Page

This one should be a no-brainer, but I'm surprised how many Etsians don't reach out to their existing friends and family, and previous and current customers, and invite them to "like" their page.

Don't worry about stepping on toes or appearing some kind of spammer. You're running an Etsy store — not selling life insurance. Most people would LOVE to get updates on how all the cool, pretty stuff your Etsy store is churning out.

Best of all, if you've got an email list you send special offers or a newsletter to, you can send them a quick email and "ask" them to become a fan of your Facebook page.

You could even do some kind of special where Fans of your page get a special discount.

Fan Booster Tip No.2: Put a "Follow Us on Facebook" Button Anywhere You Can Think Of

Doing this one thing, boosted my fan count by about 50%...huge! All you do is head over to the Facebook Developer Follow Button page and they'll spit out code for you which you can put in places such as: (here's where to do it: CraftBizInsider.com/FbookDev)

- Your e-commerce site (if you have one) Your blog (if you have one)
- Your email signature
- Your forum or message board signature
- Your "Thank you for subscribing to my email list" page

Now, if you're technically challenged, like I am, just

head over to a site like Upwork and for as little as ten dollars you can have a web programmer set it all up for you in less than a few minutes.

It's easy for them smart types.)

Fan Booster Tip No.3: Post Cool Stuff People Like and Want to Share

In the last chapter we talked about publishing the ideal content for your Facebook page. And the same principles we covered there apply here -- inspiring quotes, behind-the-scenes photos, posts that ask questions people can answer quickly.

I think it's worth noting, however, that creating content for getting shared -- and as a result getting a lot of new followers -- is about ONE SINGLE THING...making the person sharing it look special.

There's no question that much of the content you'll create for your Facebook Fan Page will be focused on tangible goals such as: Getting people to join your mailing list; Getting folks to visit your Etsy store; Getting customers to become repeat customers.

But acquiring new Facebook fans -- which helps credibility and reduces ad costs -- is done best when you put out stuff that people will look cool/hip/creative when sharing.

This includes posts that are:

- **Visual (**Hi-res Pictures and videos work best)
- **Inspiring** (Quotes, pretty pictures, motivational stuff)
- **Funny** (Share that funny photo or viral meme that's been passed on to you)
- **Questions** (The more you can get people to comment and chime in on your status updates the more opportunities you have to build your fan base.)
- **Informative how-to content**
- **Somewhat-controversial opinion**

(Nothing too dramatic -- no religion or politics -- just something that takes a different approach than the status quo)

And the cool thing about all this fan-producing content? You don't have to create ANY of it, if you don't want to.

Set up a couple of Google Alerts or scour places like AllTop or Newser and you have a good chance of finding those great piece of content -- that other people have created -- that can get your follower count up in no time.

I had an inspirational quote that brought in 500 new fans in a matter of a day. Not too shabby!

Fan Booster Tip No.4: Create Fan-Boosting Ads

We'll dig into Facebook advertising a little more in-depth in the next chapter. But for now, just realize there are many ads you can create in Facebook.

And one of the cheapest — and most-effective — Facebook ads available is what used to be called the "Click Like" ad but is now known as Engagement ads.

When setting up an engagement ad, you'll have a couple of choices:

- Post engagement - This is where you ask for Facebook's help to drive likes, shares and comments around an existing Page Post.
- Page likes - Just like it sounds. This is an ad where you try to boost the fan count of your page.
- Event response - This is when you try to get people to show that they are

"interested" or "going" to an event. (Unless you're doing a Facebook live video session or maybe doing some other live event, this may not be super-relevant.)

So, which type of ads should you create? And how much should you spend to get your Fan Count up.

Here is how I would organize it (until you reach the magical amount of 500 fans). Create two campaigns:

- **Campaign #1 Post Engagement** - Take your best post and give it a $3/day Post Engagement ad for three days
- **Campaign #2 Page Likes** - Spend $5/day for 7 days on a Page Like ad until you reach 500 fans (Which you should be able to do quite quickly)
- **Campaign #3 Post Engagement** - Take your second-best post and give it a $3/day budget for three days. (Only after your first campaign has ended.)

I know you can think of a lot more interesting ways to spend $50-$60. But after just a week, if you implement all these strategies, you'll be amazed how quickly you're able to boost your number of Facebook of fans and give your Etsy business some much-needed social proof.

Which can eventually make selling those Etsy items a heckuva lot easier. (Which IS the goal.)

Chapter 4 Action Steps:

- **Ask everybody you know to like your page.** It's okay if most won't. You just need about 25-30 to get you started.

- **Put "Follow Us on Facebook" icons everywhere.** Email signatures, Thank you pages, blogs...wherever you think would be good.

- **Post cool stuff people want to share.** Anything that makes people who share it look more hip/creative/fun/interesting will always be a big hit.

- **Create fan-boosting ads.** Spend just a couple bucks a day with post engagement ads -- those that promote a specific piece of content -- and page like ads -- those that just get your Page more likes and shares -- so you can get up to about 500 fans.

Chapter 5:
My 3-Step Facebook Ad Blueprint of Awesomeness

"Don't tell me how good you make it; tell me how good it makes me when I use it."

-Vincent van Gogh

In the next chapter I'm going to go over the EXACT nuts-and-bolts of how to create ads. (What kind of image to use? What kind of copy to write?)

But in this chapter I want to give you a big-picture look at the ad strategy that I've been using recently with real success.

And the funny part is: it's different than how

most people use ads on Facebook.

You might be a little tentative to use this strategy. It's more of a slow burn than a fast inferno of marketing.

But I've found it's more cost-effective and tends to lead to better long-term, rabid customers.

It doesn't mean this is how YOU have to use Facebook ads this way right out of the gate. Or even that you have to ever use it at all.

It's just something I've found to be extraordinarily powerful for my business. And I think it might do the same for yours.

At the end of this chapter I offer some good resources for learning how to do it. So, don't stress the details too much. Just focus on the big picture.

So, let's get into my 3-Step Facebook Ad Blueprint of Awesomeness:

Step #1: Start With a "Juicy Content" Ad

One of the big mistakes that people make when advertising on Facebook is that they ask for someone's hand in marriage on the first date.

Metaphorically, of course.

What I mean is, they ask complete strangers who've never heard of them or their Etsy store to do things like:

- Sign up for an email list
- Grab a FREE coupon
- Buy something

But imagine if you were looking for a new TV. And all of a sudden you saw an ad on your computer for the exact TV you wanted -- but from some strange company three states away you'd never heard of.

You'd be a bit wary about giving them your email address or purchasing anything.

Same applies to your would-be customers on Facebook.

You need to introduce yourself, first, before you start asking for a credit card.

And the best way to do that is to provide interesting (low-stress) content that speaks to things that interest your would-be customer.

For example, I sell Steampunk-inspired jewelry and gifts. Well, instead of badgering folks on Facebook with my ads asking them to BUY, I could instead create a piece of content on my blog or website along the lines of:

- 5 Best Steampunk Novels of 2020 You Gotta Add to Your Bookshelf
- Photo Gallery of Steampunk Baby Gift Ideas From Around the World
- Quiz: How Do You Know Which Type of Steampunk You Are?
- Debate: Jules Verne or HG Wells? Which One Is More Steampunk?

Notice how NONE of those are overtly selling

my stuff. They don't feel like sales pitches. (Unless, of course, all of the "baby gifts' were made by me.)

But they do feel like content that would resonate with my ideal audience.

Which is exactly the point.

So, here's what I recommend you do:

- Create a piece of "Juicy Content" for your ideal audience (Host it on your website)
- Promote it with a $5/day "Clicks to Website" ad (The goal is "clicks to website"; not conversions or engagement)
- Target that ad to people who are fans of your craft genre (handmade soap, candles, jewelry, art, etc.) AND who also like the "Etsy" Facebook page (Keep refining your target demographic until you have about 100k people in your ad target.)
- Keep the ad running until you get 200 or so clicks

This assumes you have that Facebook retargeting pixel installed on your website. (We went over that in Chapter 2. Head over there if you need a refresher course.)

When I start with this type of ad, instead of the usual "Buy my things now!" type of ad, I generally find more success.

Step #2: Follow It Up With a "Creative Process" Ad

I know you're just itching to get people to buy your stuff. And rightly so, you're an awesome Etsian!

But I've found it be more cost-effective to follow up that introductory "Juicy content" ad with, instead, a piece of content that tells people more about your creative process.

This could be in the form of a:

- Photo-heavy blog post
- Behind-the-scenes video
- Q&A (yes, you can ask yourself questions)

Whatever form you use, you want to share what inspires your creativity. How you got started. Why you use the materials and medium you do. And your mission as an artist. (You know, besides making cold-hard cash.)

Whenever I have skipped this crucial middle step, I've usually paid for it with a cut in sales. (Though you are welcome to go out there and prove me wrong.)

To run this type of ad you'll want to do the following:

- Create your piece of "Creative process" content (Video works great; especially if somebody with real talent can do it for you)
- Promote it with a $3/day "Clicks to Website" ad
- Target ANYBODY who landed on your website in the last three months (This includes people who clicked on your "juicy content" ad or previous customers) AND all Fans of your page (Should have at least 1,000 people to target)
- Keep running the ad until you have

about 50-100 clicks

Step #3: Close the Deal With a "Get Them to Convert" Ad

Okay, now we're ready to get down to business.

And that is by "retargeting" people who checked out your "creative process" content or already are a fan of your page and ask them to do something that directly connects to your profitability

Such as:

- Sign up for your email list
- Grab a coupon
- Check out our Etsy store
- Buy something off our website
- But something using Facebook offers (We'll go into offers in a later chapter)

What you want them to do will depend on where you are in the Etsian process.

When I was first starting out, and just had a product or two, then sending folks directly to my

ETSY store was definitely my #1 priority.

But then as I started to add items to my inventory I found that adding email subscribers actually led to more money in the long run. (Mostly because then I had more control of when I could communicate with people.)

How you approach this type of ad is very similar to the "Creative process" one. You just:

- Create a photo-rich post that asks people to act (get coupon, buy something, claim Facebook offer, sign up for email list)
- Create a "Custom Audience" of folks who checked out any page on your website OR folks who are a fan of your page
- Promote this ad with a $2/day budget

Why is this strategy so powerful?

Well, for one, the ad costs are REALLY REALLY cheap. You're only serving ads to people who already know you. Facebook knows

this and adjusts your price accordingly.

Secondly, you can just set it on auto-pilot. Have this puppy running in the background for a couple bucks a day. And after people have seen your ad for the 4th or 5th time they'll usually act. (And an action we want.)

This strategy gets even more powerful when you're able to target folks who haven't reached a particular conversion goal page.

For example, let's say you're trying to get people to sign up for your email list. And you have a page called: mywebsite.com/thank-you-email that people reach when they sign up.

Well, you simply target people who are FANS of your page or have visited at least one page on your website but have NOT reached that Thank You page.

You can do this for selling stuff straight off your website or entering contests or taking quizzes or voting for their favorite product. You can even manually upload an Excel sheet of folks who bought stuff from your Etsy store, so you remove them as well.

I know that sounded really complicated. It's not.

All you're doing is giving people who are on the fence about taking an action you desire a couple more bites at the apple. Because sometimes just a couple more opportunities is the difference between making money and having to sell off your craft supplies.

Note: I know I breezed through that pretty quickly. And it might be hard to grasp HOW this all comes together.

Here are some good resources you can use to help walk you through it:

- Creating an Ad in Facebook Business Manager (CraftBizInsider.com/FBBizAd)
- Creating a Custom Audience in Facebook (CraftBizInsider.com/FBRetargeting)

Chapter 5 Action Steps:

- **Start off with a "juicy content" ad.** This is a piece of content that would interest your ideal customer. (And does not overtly sell.

- **Follow that up with a "creative process" ad.** This is where you pull the curtain back and show your process as an artist. Talk about your mission, your influences, etc. Target people who already responded to your "juicy content" or are already Facebook fans. Avoid the hard sell...just yet.

- **Close the deal with a "get them to convert" ad.** Target Facebook fans and anybody who already visited your website. Give them a chance to claim coupons, buy exclusive stuff, sign up for your email list...whatever you want.

Chapter 6:
6 Secrets to Facebook Advertising Success

"What would life be if we had no courage to attempt anything?"

-Vincent van Gogh

There's a reason Facebook scares the HECK out of Google. Google, for all its plans of world domination — and billions of dollars in profit — lacks one HUGE thing that Facebook has...tons and tons of user data.

Facebook knows more about its one billion

users than the NSA and its spying program could ever hope to.

That's because Facebook knows what we like, what we buy and who we're friends with (and who we're not friends with).

Even scarier they can predict what we'll like, what we'll buy and the companies and people who we are inclined to connect with....before we know it ourselves!

And though this may be on the scary, big-brother side, it's a fantastic opportunity for us as Etsy sellers. Because we can use this targeted advertising to serve ads JUST to people likely to be interested in buying our wares.

NOTE: If you've tried Facebook ads in the past, and seen little success, I encourage you to give them one more try. With some small tweaks, and conservative budgets, it can be a phenomenally effective way to sell your wares.

NOTE #2: These ad strategies I'm about to suggest work best if you already have at least 500 fans for your Fan Page. If you haven't quite reached that threshold, head over to Chapter 4 where I do a deep-dive on how to create ads that boost your fan count.

So, let's jump in with my SEVEN secrets to conquering the Facebook universe with targeted ads of awesomeness:

Secret #1: Don't Stress the Low Numbers

MOST people will not click on your ad. And that's okay.

Getting a CTR (Click-thru-rate) on your ads of .4%-.5% is about average.

NOT...4 or 5%, mind you, but .4%.

But unless you are creating an ad who entire goal is engagement -- which charges the # of impressions your ad serves to strangers -- the likelihood is you'll be creating an ad that charges PER CLICK.

Which means if 100 people "see" your ad and don't click on it. You pay nothing. You only pay when somebody clicks on an ad.

Why is this distinction important?

Because studies show people often need to come in contact with a brand six or seven times before they BUY.

And with Facebook advertising, it's entirely possible to get 3-4 of those contacts for FREE, which speeds up the purchase cycle and delivers you more sales, quicker.

Secret #2: Choose the Best Type of Objective (for You)

Facebook constantly tinkers with its ad interface, so things may have changed by the time I finish typing this sentence. But what you do is click on "Create an Ad" at the upper left of your Facebook platform and choose from three key objectives.

The THREE types of objectives are:

- **Awareness** - If you want the most eyeballs and want to get your brand's name out there — and aren't concerned with conversions — this is the one you want. (Not an ideal choice for Etsians, in my opinion.)

- **Consideration** - These ads includes things like sending traffic to a website. (Such as Etsy or your own website.) Getting likes and comments to your page. Getting people to watch your video. (Probably the best option for most Etsians getting started with ads.)

- **Conversion** - Like it sounds, this type of ad is all about making sure the most likely people to convert — sign up for your email list; buy something from your WooCommerce store — will be served ads. (Probably more of an advanced approach.)

Now these all have different aims and objectives. (And slightly different learning curves.)

But here's how I would approach it:

- Engagement ads for boosting juicy content and getting page likes.
- Traffic ads for promoting your "creative process" content on your website.
- Traffic, lead generation or conversion ads

for getting people to take direct action that affects your bottom line.

Secret #3: Get a Killer Creative Photo

Here's where most Facebook ads end up failing, big-time. That's because most people click, or not to click, on an ad based on the photo.

Though this isn't an exact science, here are a few photo ad guidelines I've found to keep you on track:

- **Put people in the photo if possible**. I know you want to get your products in there but try to get somebody in there.
- **Pictures of women get the most clicks**. This is true even when women are the target audience.
- **Odd pictures work well too**. Things that are just slightly bizarre and have nothing to do with your product. I know…weird, right? But it's true.
- **Don't use logos or pictures that have text on them**. They don't work, and Facebook doesn't like them.
- **Don't use "stock images."** They look

like stock images.

- **You ARE welcome to use interesting filters** (such as exposures and tints) to make your photo stand out.
- **Ideal photo size is 1200x628**. Anything smaller and it will be resized and come out pixelated.

Before you freak out you don't know how you will resize your photo, or do anything as elaborate as adding a filter, let me introduce you to my secret Etsy weapon…PicMonkey!

PicMonkey is a FREE site — though you have to pay for advanced features — that lets you do all kinds of cool touch-ups, adjustments, and overall creative things to your photos. (Without knowing anything about Photoshop!)

Best of all, you can use PicMonkey to create all those killer photos to populate your status updates.

Secret #4: Write Awesome Ad Copy

Ah, yes, ad copy. This is one area that many Etsians freak out over. I mean, it's not like we are born copywriters…what are we supposed to say here?

Don't worry, it's easy.

Just ask questions in the headline AND sell the click in the body copy.

Now, the question you ask in the **headline** will depend on your particular Etsy emphasis.

Here are a couple of examples I like:

- Do you love handcrafts?
- Got candles?
- You a doll collector?
- Addicted to woodworking?
- Do you love yourself some steampunk?

Now, you've only got 25 characters to play with here, so you may need to come up with some different options. But keep churning them out; the more you write, the better they'll be.

And whatever you do, don't mention your Etsy store name. Nobody cares about that…yet.

As for the **body copy**, well this will depend on what the ad is designed to do. Here are a couple of templates I use:

- **Page Like ad:** "Click LIKE if you Love Decorative Candles"
- **Traffic ad:** "Check out how Steampunk fiction is inspiring this artist."
- **Facebook offer ad:** "Take 20% off your next purchase of these Etsy woodworking treasures"

Secret #5: Master the Art of Demographic Targeting

Okay, here's where things get exciting. (But where most Etsy sellers lose a ton of money.) The key with audience targeting is to make sure you aren't letting your dollars take a fast stroll out the door.

You can target your Facebook ads by:

- Location
- Age & Gender
- Precise Interests & Broad Categories (What they put down as interests.)

- Education Targeting
- Connections (Both the people and the Pages they are connected to)
- …and "More Categories" (which is as nebulous and weird as it sounds)

The absolute key to Facebook ad targeting is to test which demographics work best for your shop. (And keep tweaking things until you find that Facebook ad sweet spot.)

Here's a peek over my shoulder to see how I approach it:

- **Location** - I stick to the U.S. and Canada markets, because I tend not to ship a lot of merch overseas. (But you'll want to see what works for you best.)

- **Age & Gender** - As I mentioned earlier, I target women, ages 22-55. This is who my core demographic is. You might have a different one, but chances are as an Etsy seller your audience will skew female.

- **Precise Interests** - These interests are broad; Etsy alone has 12 million folks who name it as an interest. But it'll give you a good starting off point and can offer suggestions which will help you target further.

- **Education** - I spend little time worrying about education. You may find different results. Knock yourself out!

- **Connections** - Here's where it gets interesting. By putting down other Etsy seller Facebook pages — you can find this by using the Facebook search bar at the top — you can target fans of those pages or any other page that might be related to your creative outlet. (This targeting method, by Facebook page, is my number one best way to find new customers.)

- **More Categories** - I don't spend much time here either, none of these categories fit in with what I do. That may change.

You want to shoot for targeting specs that give you approximately 100,000 people you're able to reach with your ad.

Much more — or much less — than that and you'll be running ineffective ads that cost you money out of your pocket.

Secret #6: Set Campaign Spend

So, this will depend on what you can afford, and how quickly you want results. Below are a couple of tips to help ensure you don't lose your entire ad budget all at once:

- **Set a daily budget of about five to ten dollars** until you've got an ad that's performing well. (A CTR of about .5% means it's a winning ad.)

- **Under bidding and pricing, always "bid for clicks."** The ad impression model just doesn't work for us Etsy sellers well.

- **Set the maximum bid five cents over the "minimum suggested bid."** You'll find this info at the top left, under the audience reach section.

- **Set a start date to begin in the morning sometime**, about 6 a.m. and end a week later.

Secret #7: Test and Tweak

So I know you'd love to just "set it and forget it," but unfortunately Facebook ads don't work that way.

Keep checking in to see what's working, what's not working and how better to improve your success rate. So you get more customers, by paying less.

Now this doesn't have to take a super huge amount of time, maybe just a couple of minutes each day.

But here's what I recommend you do each day you're running a Facebook ad, to make sure you're getting the results you want (and are paying for):

- **Pause your ads in the middle of the night**. (From 10 p.m. - 6 a.m.) Facebook doesn't let you automate this, as of the time of this writing, which is annoying. But you don't want to pay for clicks when your ideal customers are asleep.

- **After 30 clicks or five days, remove any ads not getting at least .3% CTR**. Facebook charges you more for ads that don't work so well. Get rid of them as soon as you can.

- **Spin off successful ads with variations**. Any ad that gets at least a .4% CTR is average. Take that ad and change ONE element — headline, photo, copy — and see which version wins.

- **Keep tweaking and testing** until you have a solid four to five ads that kick butt.

- **Change your photos every two weeks**. People get banner blindness to see the same photos repeatedly. Mix it up and keep your ads fresh and productive.

Chapter 6 Action Steps:

- **Pick the ad you want to run**. This will be based on your goals such as getting more likes, getting more engagement for your posts or getting more visitors to check out your Etsy store or claiming a special offer.

- **Get a great ad photo created**. Pictures of real women doing something interesting — like holding your latest product — would work well.

- **Try to write a headline with a question**. Keep it simple. Make it a question your ideal customer can't say no to.

- **Write body copy with active verbs telling people what to do**. Tell 'em to "click here" and "grab it now" to get them to do what you want them to do.

- **Target the audience of your ad as much as you can**. Choosing fans of businesses similar to yours is a great way to go.

- **Set a budget of about $5-$10 a day, to get started**. Always go for clicks, not impressions.

- **Keep track of what's working and kill ads that aren't**. Slowly improving your ads is the best way to consistent traffic and a steady flow of customers.

Chapter 7:
Facebook Contests and Offers Made Easy

"All contests are unfair. You just have to win them."

-M.F. Moonzajer

Your Facebook-Etsy marketing machine should be pretty much unstoppable so far. By following the strategies we've gone over so far you should have:

- Thousands of new fans
- Tons of shares for your killer news feed content
- Lots of new folks visiting your Etsy storefront and (hopefully) becoming long-term customers

And you shouldn't have to do anything else. But things don't work out how we'd like, especially in the world of Facebook marketing.

Sometimes your Etsy store promotion efforts on Facebook need a boost, some rocket fuel to send it into the atmosphere and have it pay huge dividends down the line.

And nothing boosts your Facebook marketing like good old contests and offers. So, that's what we will cover in this chapter.

I will show you the ins and outs of these popular marketing methods which I've used to double and triple my revenue overnight.

Shall we get started?

How Facebook Offers Work

Facebook offers are web-coupons you can place on your fan page (provided you have at least 50 "likes" or fans) and send to visitors through Facebook ads, external links and any promotional tool you can dream up.

With offers you can cut out the middleman, dispense with the subtle persuasion and attract business from people in your niche market.

The reason they're so awesome is that Facebook delivers the offer email to the customer, not you!

Which boosts the probability they will redeem the offer.

And…if you do it right…you can also get a FREE email address to add your database. (Cool!)

Here's how it works:

1. **You create your Facebook offer** –much the same way you would create a Facebook ad, like we mentioned in Chapter 6. You pay a certain fee to run the offer, but this may be much more cost effective than a contest,

depending on your Etsy shop's niche. You can visit Facebook's Help Page on how to create an offer.

2.   The offer is posted on the fan page, and people sign up to take advantage of the fantabulous deal. Then, Facebook sends the offer-clicker an email.

3.   In the email, which you create, you add a link to a page on your Etsy blog or website where people can get a coupon code.

4.   On your blog, create a page with the same offer you posted on your Facebook page, and post a link to an email address. This email address can be one that is created for your Etsy shop's offers. The Facebook user follows the short instructions – and hits send.

5.   Your auto-responder moves into action, sending out a pre-written email…and furnished within the message is your *Etsy shop's coupon code*. BAM!

A couple of tips I've picked up along the about Facebook offers:

- Try to offer at least 20% off. For some reason I've had way more success with 20% off then I have with 15%. That 5% can really make a difference.

- Use a really good image. And I mean really good. If ya gotta get a pro to come take the picture, that's okay. It'll be worth it.

- Set an expiration date of seven days. You want folks to be able to share the offer with others. (They will.) But you gotta give them enough time to do it. Seven days is about right.

While this may have sounded like quite a few difficult steps, as long as you walk your customers through with clear instructions, they should have no problems getting that coupon code.

This provides a "near-seamless" way of using Facebook's Offers and Etsy's Coupon Codes – and it's automated on your end.

What do you get out of this?

Not only have you gained access to an email address for your auto-responder, allowing for you to send promo materials and even more offers – but you also just made a sale (which was the whole point in the first place).

The Beauty of Facebook Contests

I don't know what it is about a contest, maybe there's just something about the human brain that loves to play games. The cool things is: contests don't feel like marketing. (So entrants will often do the spreading and sharing for you.)

I can say the moment I ran Facebook contests, my Etsy business made significant financial gains. (Not that we're just in this for the money, mind you…)

So…how do we create a kick-butt Facebook contest? I'm so glad you asked…

Facebook Contest Step No.1: Pick Out a Prize (and What Entrants Need to Do to Win)

Finding the right prize is the absolute key to

nailing your contest. If your prize is so general —
such as an iPad — you might get a lot of contest
entrants are NOT in your ideal buying audience, but
just want to win a freebie.

Conversely, you want to make sure you have a
prize that can appeal to as large an audience as
possible. (Something like a green toilet cozy might
seem cool to you, but not everybody may agree.)

It's also important to realize that each of the
different contests require different levels of
emotional investment.

**A sweepstakes, where winners are drawn at
random, has a low barrier-to-entry, so will attract
a BIGGER pool of entrants.**

But a contest where entrants need to upload a
video or photo — or even write an essay — will get
people jazzed about your contest.

And make them more prone to share your
contest — and their contribution — with their
friends.

Say you sell creative ceramic plates with pithy

sayings on them. A *fantastic* contest idea would be to have people submit a saying of their own, and the top three would show up on your newest line of decorative plates.

Talk about making them feel like a part of the process.

In addition, the top three entrants might receive a free ceramic plate with their own saying on it.

Or you might do something where entrants send in a sample of their own artwork, antiques, projects, etc., and you give the winning photo a free $30 gift certificate for your Etsy shop.

Believe me, it'll be the best $30 you ever spend.

Now, in my experience, I've had the biggest successes with the "photo" and "short essay" forms of contests.

I find the video contests scares people away, with its technological hurdles, and that sweepstakes contests just attract a lot of freeloaders.

Try a couple different contest forms and see what works for you.

Facebook Contest Step No.2: Play by the (Facebook) Rules

This tip is an easy decision, and yet many marketers (including huge brands) will run these amazing Facebook contests that violate the Facebook terms of service.

You can check out their complete rules under the "promotions" section at CraftBizInsider.com/FbookPolicy.

There are rules about the ages of contestants, advertising for the event, etc.

But the most important rule is to make sure you don't imply, at all, that *Facebook is involved with your contest.*

Know these guidelines and know them well. Please do this because bad things can happen to good people.

I know of fellow Etsians who've had their Facebook account banned because they didn't follow contest guidelines; don't let this happen to you.

Facebook Contest Step No.3: Pick an App to Handle the Contest

Apps make life easy, and that proves doubly true with contests.

A contest app will:

1. Handle all the administrative back-end contest stuff you don't want to do. (Trust me.)
2. Make sure every aspect of your contest is mobile-friendly. (This is big!)
3. Offer you some great tools to help promote your contest.

Now, unfortunately most of the great contest apps are NOT free. But the ones I recommend below are all worth the money, and I've ALWAYS seen phenomenal results when I've tried them.

Here are my faves:

1. **WooBox** is a larger utility, which runs a series of smaller contest apps. Offering a diverse set of tools, WooBox can help your Facebook contest get off the ground —because these apps keep things simple for the contestants.

2. Easy Promos is nice because it offers a free trial, which is often one problem with other apps. Especially if you are a newbie on Facebook contests, Easy Promos may just be the ticket.

3. ShortStack is nice because you can use this app to customize your own Facebook fan page to suit the contest. It's also reasonably priced.

*Ah, one more thing: make sure that your guidelines, rules and steps are clear and concise.

For instance, if you want to offer something from your Etsy store, but you don't want the winner to walk away with a $200-item… then state you will only allow a freebie of $50 or less.

Facebook Contest Step No.4: Promote Your Contest Everywhere You Can Think Of

And I mean EVERYWHERE! This includes:

- On your Facebook page
- On your Facebook personal profile
- On your personal blog and/or website
- All of your social platforms, such as

Twitter, LinkedIn, Tumblr.
- On video sharing sites such as YouTube and Vimeo
- In your email and forum signatures
- In any newsletters or promotional emails you send out
- Press releases (Easier and cheaper than you'd think)

Just share it in every place you can think of and soon momentum will build and the whole contest will take off like you never dreamed.

Chapter 7 Action Steps:

- **Create a few Facebook offers and see how they do**. Target them like your regular Facebook ads and create a landing page to gather the email address.

- **Come up with a cool contest you could run**. Select a cool prize, and what entrants need to do to win. (Photos and quick text contributions have worked best for me.)

- **Read the Facebook rules regarding contests and sweepstakes**. There aren't many, but you need to know them.

- **Choose a contest Facebook app service**, such as Woobox, to run the back-end of your contest. It'll be worth it, trust me.

- **Promote your contest as much as you can**. That includes your website, your Fan Page and all your social media platforms.

Chapter 8:
The Powerful (and Sometimes Scary) World of Facebook Live Videos

"We are afraid to care too much, for fear that the other person does not care at all."

-Eleanor Roosevelt

The only thing scarier than presenting yourself (and your crafts) on video might just be presenting yourself (and your crafts) on LIVE video.

And if the thought of hitting "Record" on your iPhone app brings up some trepidation — and more than a little dread — then let me just say I feel your pain.

I might feel comfortable in the confines of my craft room. Or talking to you now through some ramblings on my laptop.

But the prospect of talking to people LIVE on camera filled me with so much anxiety that I thought about deleting the Facebook app from my computer. (Just so I wouldn't have to think about it.)

But there were a few compelling reasons I pushed through my resistance and gave this fascinating (if terrifying) new tool a try:

- **Facebook really wants it to work.** Facebook is coming after YouTube with everything it has. And with Facebook Live they are trying really hard to make their platform the hub for online video. Which means they will promote the heck out of your video, if you use their tool.

- **Great way to connect with audience.** With the ability for viewers to ask questions in real-time it's a fantastic way to get feedback and find out what your viewers REALLY think.

- **Boosts the popularity of your Facebook pages.** Feel like your Facebook page needs some re-charging. Do a Facebook Live session and you'll see engagement rates skyrocket more than 1000%.

- **Perfect for product releases.** This is probably my favorite way to use Facebook Live. If I have a new creation coming out, I'll usually do a quick 20-minute video unveiling it and talking about the inspiration for it.

So, if I haven't completely scared you off yet — and you are mildly intrigued by the prospect of doing some Facebook Live video content — here are FIVE strategies to ensure your next Facebook Live session is as effective as it can be.

Strategy #1: Promote That Sucker Early

You want to start promoting your live video event as soon as possible. Because that's exactly what it is. A live event.

This means doing things like:

- Posting daily updates about the live event
- Sharing tidbits about topics you'll cover in the live event
- Promote on other social channels (and message boards)
- Create a Facebook ad promoting the event (this can work like gangbusters)

Strategy #2: Create a Good Shooting Environment

Before you stroll over to your craft room and fire up the old smartphone to start your event, it's important that you get some basics set up, so things go as smoothly as you'd like.

A couple of important details include:

- **A non-distracting background.**
  Remember that famous video of Sarah
  Palin stumping on the campaign trail as
  a man decapitated a turkey in the
  background. Though I doubt you'll have
  such a dramatic background for your
  video, you'll still want to make sure your
  background has neutral colors and no
  distracting imagery.

- **Have good audio.** You may think
  quality video is the most important
  element of a Facebook Live event. But
  without good audio your event will be
  unwatchable. Make sure you've got an
  external mic, or some kind of audio
  device, besides your camera's built-in
  microphone so you can sound as good
  as possible.

- **Check the lighting.** Here's the rule
  about lighting: Have the light behind the
  camera, focused on the subject.
  Shooting into light, even sunlight, can
  make everything dark and quite difficult

to see.

- **Choose vertical or horizontal.** If you're shooting your Facebook Live video with a smartphone, you'll have to decide whether you shoot horizontally — phone on its side — or vertically — phone upright. I usually go with horizontal; shows off my craft room better and doesn't make me look too close to the camera. But test things out to see what works for your event.

- **Record when people are ready to watch.** When should you schedule your Facebook Live event? Well, I can't give you an absolute rule. But for me late afternoons/early evenings on Thursday are perfect. But this will depend on when your ideal customer is up and around.

Strategy #3: Stay in the Moment

I am by no means a professional performer

when it comes to being on camera. But here are a couple of hacks I've used to help me stay grounded and perform to the best of my abilities.

- **Pretend like you're talking to one person.** I know you're not. But try to imagine what your ideal customer would look like. Give her or him a name. And picture them in your mind as you perform. It will not only help you through the jitters but make your performance better.

- **Keep reminding people what they're watching.** This one took me awhile to figure out. But it's an old radio trick. And because you don't know when people are coming in and coming out you want to remind people of what's going on. "In case you're just joining us…I'm showing you all how to make a Steampunk Darth Vader tree ornament. First we got the soldering iron." Don't worry about being repetitive. It'll just help everybody watching. Even those who are there from the beginning.

- **Try to address comments and questions as they come up.** This can be a challenge the first couple times you do it. ("Talking to a camera is hard enough. You mean I also gotta read at the same time?") But your engagement will sky-rocket if you're able to respond to viewer's feedback in a relatively short amount of time. It not only makes people who asked questions feel good but inspires other folks to ask questions as well.

Strategy #4: Follow Up With Some Follow-Up

The moment your Facebook Live video event is done it will be archived in the Facebook vaults for posterity.

Which means you can re-purpose it again and again on different platforms.

A couple of the ways I re-use my videos:

- A "Thanks for joining me" post on Facebook in which you tag folks who asked questions.

- A "Got any questions we missed?" post on Facebook in which you link to your Facebook Live video, as well as ask for any other questions/comments.

- Spotlight notable comments from viewers. Just pull out any notable comments or questions and feature them in an ongoing Facebook discussion.

- Pull out notable comments/questions and feature them on Twitter.

- Get a transcript of your video done and publish it on your blog. (Great way to get some extra SEO wonderfulness headed your website's way.)

- Use your past Facebook Live video to

promote your next one. This gives a sneak preview of what people might see if they watch.

I know all this Facebook Live talk might be freaking you out.

That's okay. It freaked me out.

Just let it marinate in your mind for a bit and see if you can be open to the possibility of doing a live event.

And maybe after your fear and loathing have subsided you might just give this most-powerful tool a chance to not just connect with fans and followers…but embed your creations in the mind of would-be customers around the world.

Chapter 8 Action Steps:

- **Promote that sucker early.** Post daily updates and share interesting tidbits about what you got planned for your Facebook Live video event.

- **Create a good shooting environment.** Make sure the lighting is behind the camera, that you have a non-distracting background, good audio, and an effective time for your Facebook Live session to reach the most people.

- **Stay in the Moment.** You can do this by pretending like you're talking to one person, address comments as they come up, and keep reminding people who you are and what you're talking about.

- **Follow up with follow-up.** Give a shout out to anybody who had comments or asked questions. Re-purpose your event by pulling out specific topics as well as using it to promote your next event.

Chapter 9:
How to Assemble Your
Facebook Marketing Team

"Alone we can do so little. Together we can do so much."

-Helen Keller

I know you feel like this whole Facebook marketing thing will take you forever to master.

That it'll take you months before you get the hang of posting content that gets shared a ton and years before you figure out how to run profitable and cost-effective ad campaigns that help you sell your latest creations while you sleep.

Trust me: spend about five to ten minutes a day just trying stuff out with your Facebook page — and tweaking to make small improvements — and before you know it, you'll be an absolute pro.

The only limitations you'll have will be your available time and energy. And social media marketing can cut in time better spent on creating more Etsy products and…sleeping.

So, that's what we will talk about this in rather brief chapter.

I will show you how to off-load some of your Facebook marketing duties to other people, at little to no cost to your bottom line, and how to leverage other people's sweat equity to help turn your quaint Etsy business into an online craft giant.

Facebook Team Tip No.1: Find a (Somewhat) Professional Photographer

I know what you're saying: "A photographer? What's that got to do with Facebook?"

Well, as Etsy sellers, we all know the power of a powerful product photo. It can boost our sales and maximize our brand profile.

Not to mention make us look professional even if we're just making our stuff in the laundry room.

GREAT photos can make the job of marketing on Facebook easy.

Though I know you THINK your iPhone photos are just fine, and that you've had good results with them, there's just something about elegant photos taken by somebody who knows what they're doing with a camera that can do absolute wonders with your business.

So, if you haven't already, try to schedule time at least once or twice a month for a sharp photographer to come out to where your Etsy magic happens and takes some amazing photos of:

- New or recurring products
- Your Etsy workstation
- Action shots of you and your team
- Anything involving cats, dogs, or babies (People frickin' love those)
- Close-ups of anything with your Etsy store name on it

Now you don't have to get a $1000 per-hour photographer on the payroll. I contact my local junior college and ask if any talented photography students want to come out for an hour and make an extra $50-$100.

Trust me, they will.

And worry not about the expense, by getting some amazing photos taken you can charge MORE money because the perceived value of your products will be higher.

Cool, right?

Facebook Team Tip No.2: Find Intern to Handle Content Duties

One of the biggest time sucks you'll encounter with Facebook is finding cool "stuff" to post on Facebook and posting that "stuff."

Which is why it's the perfect gig for a young, ambitious — but poor — college student intern.

Now I don't believe in indentured servitude, so I would pay your intern SOMETHING. (I have an intern who I pay $75 bucks for about eight to ten hours of work a week.)

So, unless you're living in a bomb shelter miles underground, somewhere in your community will be a young person who wants to get college credit and valuable real-world business experience.

That you run an Etsy store will be even cooler.

And what do you have this intern do? Well, anything you feel they'd be up for:

- Searching the web for fun, interesting content
- Collecting motivational quotes
- Editing and resizing your photos in PicMonkey
- Scheduling all your posts way in advance
- Interacting with comments on the Facebook Fan Page

I've even had interns who shot video for me — because that's what they were into. But you must adjust the duties to the skills of the intern.

I have to say, some of my most rewarding business experiences have been with interns who've brought great ideas to my Etsy business.

Facebook Team Tip No.3: Find a Social Media Manager

Once you've had experience with an intern taking some daily grind duties off your plate, it might be a time to broaden out your social media team.

And the best way to do that is to find a dedicated social media manager to add to your Etsy empire.

Now, this is NOT a full-time position. (Unless you've gotten Facebook Fan Pages you're juggling.)

However, you need somebody more reliable and professional than a college intern looking for some extra burrito money.

I have my VA (Virtual Assistant) or Social Media Manager handle things like:

- Creating my ads
- Collecting ad performance reports
- Pausing and restarting my ads
- Creating my special offers

- Handling the details of my contests
- Updating my blog
- Uploading my new product photos to my Etsy store
- Whatever I need done!

The best places I've found this part-time, but skilled, labor is on freelance sites such as Upwork. There you can find talented, but unemployed, folks dying to help you out.

Of the two, Upwork is the cheapest, and it skews more toward contractors who are abroad. (I've had great success with virtual assistants in the Philippines.)

But post ads in both places, letting them know what you're looking for, and you're likely to find a great addition to your team that will save you a ton of time and make you more money in the long run.

Chapter 9 Action Steps:

- **Hire a photographer to shoot your latest products** and your colorful work station at least once or twice a month. Great places to find these photogs would be your local junior college or university.

- **Bring an intern into your fold to handle some daily Facebook Fan Page maintenance**. A good intern can handle all your content collection and post scheduling. (Be sure to pay them; this isn't czarist Russia.)

- **When you're ready, hire a VA (Virtual Assistant)** to handle the more delicate areas of your Facebook marketing efforts. VA's are perfect for handling all your advertising tests, contest details, and any day-to-day administrative duties that will give you more time to focus on your Etsy creations.

A Final Word

"Success is stumbling from failure to failure without a loss of enthusiasm."

-Winston Churchill

Not everything you do in regards to Facebook marketing will work. In fact, I'm pretty confident in saying most of what you try won't be a rousing success.

o   You'll create posts on your Fan Page that only you and your second cousin will read.

o   You'll send out special offers that illicit all the excitement of an IRS audit.

    o   You'll painstakingly manage ad campaigns that are about as successful as a Mitt Romney presidential bid.

But — and here's the big lesson I wish somebody had told me years back — try to learn JUST one small thing from your marketing efforts each day. It doesn't have to be huge or monumental.

Maybe it's that short quotes get shared more than long quotes. (Which is true.) Maybe it's that Sunday nights are great for Facebook engagement, but Friday nights are like a ghost town. (Which is also true.)

Or maybe it's just that your community of Facebook fans REALLY like it when you share photos of your dog, or pictures of your favorite tea or rant about the rudeness of people on cell phones. (Which I'm willing to bet is true.)

Because as busy as our lives are in this crazy, smartphone world of ours …anything that can remind us to slow down and appreciate the little things people will respond to.

And if you put your heart into your Facebook fan page, and post content that people feel emotional and passionate about you'll find your Etsy business growing in ways you never thought possible.

I wish you luck in your future Etsy marketing endeavors, and if you'd like to drop me a line, just ping me over at charles@craftbizinsider.com.

A Special FREE Gift for You!

If you'd like FREE instant access to my special report "Top 10 Marketing Tools Every Etsy Seller Should Use" then head over to **CraftBizInsider.com/Free**.

(What else you gonna do? Watch another "Twilight" movie?!)

DISCLAIMER AND/OR LEGAL NOTICES:
Every effort has been made to accurately represent this book and it's potential. Results vary with every individual, and your results may or may not be different from those depicted. No promises, guarantees or warranties, whether stated or implied, have been made that you will produce any specific result from this book. Your efforts are individual and unique, and may vary from those shown. Your success depends on your efforts, background and motivation.

The material in this publication is provided for educational and informational purposes only and is not intended as business advice. Use of the programs, advice, and information contained in this book is at the sole choice and risk of the reader.

Printed in Great Britain
by Amazon